USING THE PANEL
IN TEACHING AND TRAINING

LEROY FORD

Illustrated by Joe McCormick
Based on author's original sketches

BROADMAN PRESS ♦ Nashville, Tennessee

© 1970 • Broadman Press
Nashville, Tennessee
All rights reserved
ISBN: 0–8054–4234–14

Dewey Decimal Classification Number: 268.6
Library of Congress Catalog Card Number: 79–127196
Printed in the United States of America
7.5AT7018

Contents

The search for a way to express learning theory and techniques in an interesting, readable style led to the development of the cartooned-writing approach used in this and other books by the author. Most readers agree that they grasp and retain ideas better when the ideas receive exaggerated or absurd treatment through cartooning.

Most of the cartoons in this book found expression first as stick figures. Sometimes the stimulation of a class or conference session gave rise to an idea which the author later translated into stick-figure cartoons on the chalkboard. Sometimes ideas came from personal and family experiences. Significant statements in books sometimes suggested humorous nonverbal ways to express ideas.

"Cartooned writing" seeks to carry through pictures the weight of a message. Verbal symbols (words) added to the cartoons help clarify meanings and provide continuity of thought.

I wish to express appreciation to artist Joe McCormick for his assistance in sharpening the original cartoons. Phyllis Gregory kept the project moving and made helpful suggestions for improving the manuscript.

*Multi-Media Publications by LeRoy Ford

Number 1: *Primer for Teachers and Leaders*
Number 2: *Using the Lecture in Teaching and Training*
Number 3: *Using the Case Study in Teaching and Training*
Number 4: *Using the Panel in Teaching and Training*

Other Books by the Author

Tools for Teaching and Training
Developing Skills for Church Leaders

*Multi-Media publications are available in book, filmstrip, and chart set format.

4

"PANEL"

MEANS DIFFERENT THINGS TO DIFFERENT PEOPLE

To the bread man
it means . . .

... HIS TRUCK!

To a beauty contestant
it means . . .

. . . THE JUDGES!

To a person on trial
it means . . .

... THE JURORS!

To an astronaut
it means . . .

...THE INSTRUMENT "BOARD"

To the cabinetmaker
it means . . .

But to the teacher—or trainer—
it means . . .

LET'S DEFINE
THE
PANEL

A panel is . . .

AN INSTRUCTIONAL METHOD IN WHICH

SEVERAL PERSONS

DISCUSS AMONG THEMSELVES

BEFORE AN AUDIENCE

THE VARIOUS FACETS OF A PROBLEM,

WITH LEADERSHIP

A panel is an instructional method in which . . .
several persons . . .

discuss *among themselves* . . .

. . . with **leadership.**

Now. . . . Let's *you* define panel!

A PANEL IS: ____ _____

_____ ____ _____

SEVERAL _____ ____

_____ _____ BEFORE

_____ _____ _____

FACETS ___ __ _____)

_____ _____ .

19

The panel encourages free exchange of ideas . . .

. . . instead of formal speeches.

Panel members carry on an informal discussion *as if* the audience *were not there!*

But the audience *is* there!

And you don't have to have a table! . . .

. . . but it sometimes helps!

A panel *is not* a seated symposium!

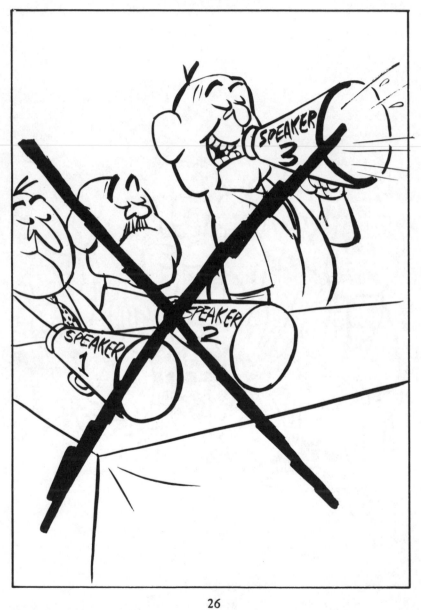

Others define panel this way . . .

1. A panel consists of a small number of people who "discuss" something. (Hoover)

2. A small group of experts or well-informed persons discuss a problem for the benefit of an audience. (Holbert and Gulley)

3. A type of conference situation taking place in a face-to-face setting, generally informal in procedure, usually held before the audience, and employing as its chief method a free interchange among participants rather than prepared, formal speeches. (Settle and Miller)

4. The panel sets up an audience (panel nucleus) within an audience (the listening members) and hopes to fuse the two groups into a single reflective unit. (Baird)

5. Three or more resource persons engaged in a purposeful conversation on an assigned subject. (Williams)

6. One form of discussion is the panel, in which from three to six people informally discuss some subject with one another under the guidance of a moderator or panel leader who introduces the subject and helps keep the discussion on the track. (Little)

7. A group of four to eight persons who have special knowledge of the topic sit at a table in front of the audience and hold an orderly and logical conversation on the assigned topic. (Bergevin and Morris)

Now test your understanding!

Which of the following statements best illustrates the panel?

1. Mr. Chandler planned a unit of study on the theme "Baptists in early America." He decided to emphasize the contributions of three outstanding Baptists: John Leland, Isaac Backus, and William Screven. For the session, he asked three members to sit behind a table at the front of the room. He asked one to speak for five minutes on "Contributions of John Leland"; another to speak on "Contributions of Isaac Backus." The other he asked to speak on "Contributions of William Screven." After the presentations, he asked the audience to ask questions of the three members.

2. Mrs. Henderson planned a study session on "The Influence of John Leland, the Baptist, on American History." She enlisted three group members to assist. At the beginning of the session, she announced that the three members would discuss the problem, Would the Bill of Rights have included guarantees of religious liberty aside from the influence of John Leland? Why or why not? The three members talked informally about the pros and cons of the problem. Then Mrs. Henderson summarized the arguments for and against the idea.

3. Mr. Bailey asked three youths to do background study on "Baptists in Early America." Other group members studied a brief article on the subject. At the beginning of the session, he asked group members to ask questions of the three who had done specialized study. Then he summarized the discussion.

3. No, members did not discuss among themselves.
2. Yes
1. No, this is not a symposium-forum.

28

PANELS SERVE MANY PURPOSES

Teachers and trainers use the panel to . . .

1. Identify and *clarify* problems

2. Present various *points of view*

3. Analyze the *advantages* and disadvantages of a course of action

4. Give the feeling of popular *participation*

5. Consider problems about which the larger group is *uninformed*

6. *Pave* the way for large group discussion

7. Arrive at a *synthesis* of opinion

8. Give the "appearance of *acceptance*" of a viewpoint

9. Provide practice in cooperative *problem solving*

10. Discuss problems rather than *topics*

(Note: In each of these statements a key word is italicized. On page 42 you will be asked to recall these statements using the key words as prompts.)

1. Teachers and leaders use the panel to identify and clarify problems.

2. Teachers and leaders use the panel to present various points of view.

3. We can use the panel to analyze advantages and disadvantages of a course of action.

4. We can use the panel to give the feeling of popular participation.

In other words, it makes everybody get in on the act—through identification with persons and points of view.

5. Teachers and trainers use the panel to consider problems about which the larger group is uninformed—to extend to many the insights of a few.

6. We use the panel to pave the way for large group discussion.

7. Sometimes we use the panel to help us arrive at a synthesis of opinion.

8. Some use the panel to give the "appearance of acceptance" of a viewpoint.

9. We can use the panel to provide practice in co-operative problem solving.

10. Panels discuss problems rather than topics.

Now test your memory.

(Look at the key words below. Then write in the blank the purposes of the panel as suggested by the key word.)

Key Word	Statement
1. Clarify	_____
2. Points of view	_____
3. Advantages	_____
4. Participation	_____
5. Uninformed	_____
6. Pave	_____
7. Synthesis	_____
8. Acceptance	_____
9. Problem Solving ..	_____
10. Topics	_____

WE CAN USE THE PANEL IN MANY FORMS

Variations of the panel include . . .

1. The double panel (colloquy)

2. Panel groups within a larger group

3. Panel with a leadership team

4. Dramatized panel

5. Dispersed panel

1. The double panel* gets closer to the audience.

* Usually called the colloquy.

45

In the double panel . . .

... DISCUSSES A PROBLEM
WITH A "PANEL"
OF EXPERTS.

2. Some teachers and trainers use *panel groups*, each of which serves as a panel.

3. We can use a leadership team with the panel.

The recorder assists the moderator by reviewing the data presented by panel members—when called upon.

The resource person verifies facts and gives expert opinion when called upon.

The process observer assists the moderator evaluating how panelists work together.

A work arrangement similar to the double panel works well.

4. Sometimes we use the dramatized panel. The panel members wear costumes and discuss in an appropriate setting.

5. In the dispersed panel, panel members stand at strategic places in the audience.

Look at these pictures. Then in the blanks identify the form of panel each picture illustrates.

1._____

_____

2._____

_____

3._____

_____

4._____

_____

5._____

_____

EFFECTIVE MODERATORS*
PROMOTE
MEANINGFUL DISCUSSION

* OR LEADERS
OR CHAIRMEN
OR CONVENERS

Effective panel moderators . . .

1. Lead in planning discussion outlines in advance

2. State the discussion problem clearly

3. Establish a "conversational climate"

4. Brief panel members on what to expect of the audience

5. Balance the talkative and nontalkative members

6. Prevent "tangential meandering"

7. Practice objectivity; avoid taking sides

8. Spread audience participation

9. Lead generalizers to be specific

10. Wear many hats; play many roles

> He is: Mr. Peacemaker
> Mr. Summarizer
> Mr. Relaxer
> Mr. Prober
> Mr. Clarifier
> Mr. Decentralizer
> Mr. Navigator

1. **Effective moderators lead in planning discussion outlines in advance.**

2. Effective moderators state the problem clearly.

Give this idea a thought or two!

"A PROBLEM
WELL-DEFINED
IS
HALF SOLVED!"

JOHN DEWEY

"THE MERE
FORMULATION
OF A PROBLEM
IS FAR MORE
OFTEN ESSENTIAL
THAN ITS
SOLUTION..."

ALBERT EINSTEIN

3. Moderators establish a casual conversational climate . . .

4. Good moderators brief panel members on what to expect of the audience.

5. Tactful moderators balance the talkative and non-talkative members.

6. Effective moderators prevent "rabbit chasing."

. . . If you prefer a more sophisticated term . . . he prevents . . .

7. Good moderators both encourage and practice objectivity; avoid taking sides.

Some moderators find it difficult to hide their own prejudices

8. An effective moderator
spreads audience participation . . .

THIS:

... NOT THIS:

9. A good moderator leads the generalizer to be specific.

10. A skillful moderator wears many hats!

Among his many roles are . . .

Mr. Peacemaker

Mr. Prober

Mr. Clarifier

Mr. Navigator

Mr. Decentralizer

Mr. Summarizer

Mr. Relaxer

He is Mr. Peacemaker.

He is . . .
    Mr. Prober

(He gets to the bottom of things!)

He learns to use the question . . .

He is . . .
 Mr. Clarifier

(He brings things into focus.)

He is . . .
    Mr. Navigator

He is Mr. Decentralizer.

(He breaks up conversation "cliques.")

He is . . .
  Mr. Summarizer.

He is Mr. Relaxer.

Let's take an open-book test!

Each of the following cases illustrates a moderator employing one of the guidelines you have studied. Put your finger at page 58 so you can refer to it easily. Then read each of these cases. Write in the blank the number of the appropriate guidelines shown on page 58.

Guideline Number: *Case:*

_____ 1. A moderator said during the forum period, "We have not heard from anyone on the right front of the room. Does someone there have a question or wish to comment?"

_____ 2. In a presession planning session, the moderator and panel members composed four problem statements the panel would deal with.

_____ 3. At the beginning of the session, the moderator displayed a chart showing the four problem statements. He read them aloud.

_____ 4. The moderator, in a briefing session, told the panel members that they would best use nontechnical language since the educational level of the audience members was relatively low.

_____ 5. A moderator commented during the session, "I'm sure we're all interested in those interesting experiences. I wonder, however, if in view of our time limitations we can look again at our problem.

_____ 6. Mr. Johnson, sensing that the atmosphere was tense, told a humorous story related to the situation. The panel members and the audience laughed together.

_____ 7. The moderator sat in a chair at the front of the room. Addressing panel member number one he said, "John, tell our audience about your most embarrassing moment."

WE CAN COMBINE THE PANEL WITH OTHER METHODS

Teachers and trainers combine the panel method with such other methods as . . .

1. Panel-forum

2. Small study groups

3. Listening teams

4. Case studies

5. Role playing

6. Problem solving

1. Most teachers and trainers use the forum with the panel. (*panel-forum*)

2. We can ask *small study groups* to react to a panel or to prepare questions for a forum period.

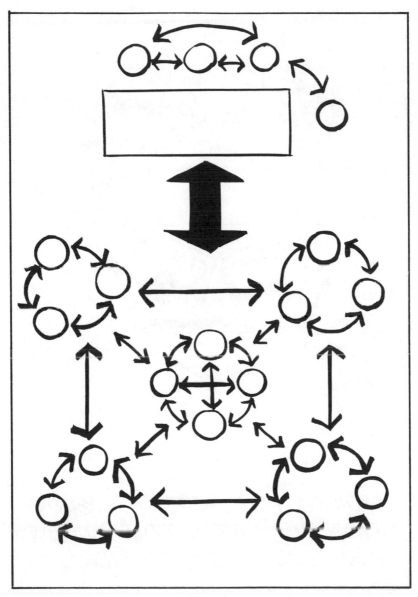

3. *Listening teams* focus one's "intent" to learn.

4. We can present *case studies* for panel members to analyze.

5. Panel members and audience alike respond to problems presented through the *role play*.

6. When time permits, panel members can use the steps in *problem solving* as a guide.

Now "read" these pictures.
For each of the pictures below, indicate the learning method it suggests for use with the panel.

1._____

_____

2._____

_____

3._____

_____

4._____

_____

5._____

_____

6._____

_____

EFFECTIVE PANEL MEMBERS FOLLOW GUIDELINES, TOO!

Effective panel members follow guidelines like these . . .

1. Know the subject; have something worth saying

2. Limit appropriately their remarks

3. Talk without prodding

4. Avoid irrelevant ideas and discourses

5. Speak up so as to be heard

6. Learn to say "I don't know"

7. Avoid technical terms

8. Organize their ideas

9. Cite sources when necessary

10. Look for the forest as well as the trees

11. Play helping roles as in any group discussion

1. A panel member must know his subject!

   His first three qualifications are:

1. HE MUST HAVE SOMETHING TO SAY!

2. HE MUST HAVE SOMETHING TO SAY!

3. HE MUST HAVE SOMETHING TO SAY!

A PANEL MEMBER CAN
NO MORE TALK ABOUT
WHAT HE DOESN'T KNOW

THAN COME BACK
FROM WHERE HE
HASN'T BEEN !

2. Good panelists limit their remarks. They use the "kiss" formula!

3. Good panelists talk without prodding.

"LET EACH ONE SERVE
THE GROUP TO THE
MEASURE OF HIS
ENDOWMENT,
AS HELPFUL
MANAGERS OF GOD'S
RICHLY VARIED GRACE."

(I PETER 4:10,
BERKELEY)

4. Effective panelists avoid irrelevant ideas! They *don't* follow this example.

What Do I Expect to Get Out of This Course?

In answer to the question What Do I Expect to Get Out of This Course? which is the subject of our theme for today, the answer is that I expect to get a great deal out of this course and I hope my work will be satisfactory in it. I realize that all students should take this course, because it is very important that all educated people should be able to fluently write good English.

This is very important, because when a person gets out of college afterwards and cannot write good English in letters or reports, or maybe he wants to become a writer, then people will think he has not been properly educated. Somebody famous has said that the mark of being a fully educated man is good writing, and I certainly agree with that. By writing a daily theme every day I am bound to become better at writing them, because, as the old saying goes, practice makes perfect.

It is the same way in everything. Look at that run Magruder made in the last game last fall. They had the game sewed up, as the sports writers say, and nobody gave us a chance to beat them, because they had beaten everybody all fall. Then Magruder ran seventy-two yards for a touchdown; some people say it was seventy-three.

The point of this is that I am not saying Magruder isn't a great back, because he is and the sports writers were crazy not to put him on the All-American, but the point is that if he had not practiced all fall hard, he could not have made this run.

That is why I say that practice makes perfect, and why I expect by the time the trees are again in bloom and the birds are caroling that I will have become a fluent writer, because, as somebody has said, there is no use of having good ideas if you cannot express them.

That is the point about Magruder. Lots of other halfbacks know that it is a good idea to run seventy-five yards for a touchdown, but the idea is to do it—that is, express the idea. That is what Magruder did, and that is what I hope to do. I don't mean making a seventy-five yard run but writing excellent English from What I Have Got Out of This Course.*

* Reprinted by special permission from the *Saturday Evening Post*, by The Curtis Publishing Company.

5. Effective panel members organize their ideas.

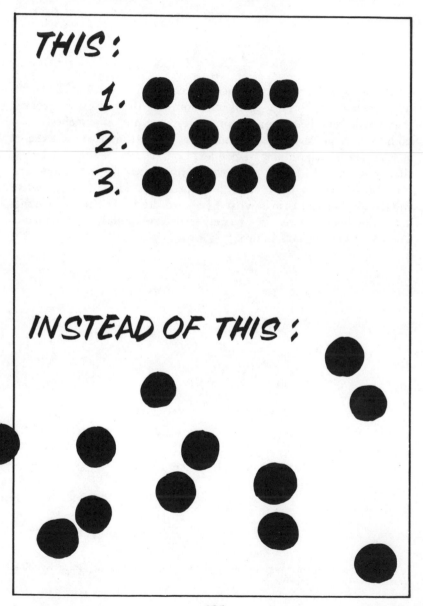

6. Thoughtful panel members avoid technical terms.

7. Panel members play even *more* roles than the moderators.

1. Mr. Information-Giver
2. Mr. Relaxer
3. Mr. Evaluator
4. Mr. Prober
5. Mr. Information-Seeker
6. Mr. Summarizer
7. Mr. Clarifier
8. Mr. Encourager
9. Mr. Mediator
10. Mr. Navigator
11. Mr. Decentralizer

Match each of these statements with the appropriate "name" on the opposite page.

_____ "I believe that Harry really meant that . . ."

_____ "Did you hear the story about the man who . . . ?"

_____ "John, from your experience you may be able to interpret for Raymond the . . ."

_____ "All this sounds good but could we look again at our discussion problem?"

_____ "Up to this point we have said that . . ."

_____ "Perhaps we are not as far apart at it appears. What common denominators of truth do you see in each approach?"

_____ "But _why?_ What do you mean by that?"

_____ "I appreciate John's good preparation for this discussion."

_____ "We've already achieved two of our goals fairly satisfactorily; but I feel we have not done so well on this problem."

"Who recalls the population of Dallas?"

Answers: 7,2,11,10,6,9,1,4,8,3,5

109

8. The best of panel members must learn to admit, "I just don't know"—at times.

THE AUDIENCE NEEDS GUIDELINES, TOO!

1. Write out your questions for the forum period.

2. Wait for recognition from the moderator.

3. Keep to the primary issues. Avoid wasting time on "molehill" issues.

4. Address the moderator first even when specifying a particular panel member.

AND SPEAKING OF P'S...

PANELS OFTEN CHANGE

PASSIVE
PUPILS INTO

PURPOSEFUL

PARTICIPANTS!

PLAN A PANEL!

Book Summary

The word "panel" means different things to different people. To the bread man it means his truck. To a beauty contestant it means the judges. To a person on trial it means the jurors. To an astronaut it means the instrument "board." To a cabinetmaker it means a slab of oak or pine or cedar.

Let's Define "Panel"

To the teacher and trainer it means:

> An instructional method in which several persons discuss among themselves, before an audience, the various facets of a problem—with leadership.

The panel encourages free exchange of ideas instead of formal speeches. Panel members carry on an informal discussion *as if* the audience were not there—but it *is* there! Panel members do not even have to sit behind a table! A panel *is not* a seated symposium.

Panels Serve Many Purposes

1. Teachers and leaders use the panel to *identify and clarify* problems.

2. Teachers and leaders use the panel *to present various points of view.* Mrs. Get-It-From-the-Bakers, Mrs. Make-It-From-Scratch and Mrs. Ready-Mix could well present different points of view on the problem, What is the best way to provide cake for the family.

3. We use the panel *to analyze advantages and disadvantages of a course of action.*

4. We can use the panel *to give the feeling of popular participation.* In other words it makes everybody get in on the act—through identification with persons and points of view.

5. Teachers and trainers use the panel *to consider problems about which the larger group is uninformed.* Panel members can extend to many the insights of a few.

6. We use the panel *to pave the way for large group discussion*. The panel takes on added meaning when followed by large group discussion in a forum.

7. Sometimes we use the panel *to help us arrive at a synthesis of opinion*.

8. Some use the panel *to give the "appearance of acceptance" of a viewpoint*. However, panels lose much of their educational validity when used for manipulative purposes.

9. We can use the panel *to provide practice in cooperative problem solving*. Problem solving involves (1) stating the problem, (2) getting the facts, (3) determining posible solutions, (4) selecting the best solution, (5) and taking action.

10. Panels *discuss problems rather than topics*. For example, instead of discussing the topic "Drug Use in Bellville," the panel would discuss the problem What Causes Drug Abuse? How can we combat it in Bellville?

We Can Use the Panel in Many Forms

1. The *double panel* (usually called the colloquy) gets closer to the audience. In the double panel or colloquy, a "panel" of audience representatives discusses a problem with a "panel" of experts. The double panel proves especially effective when the audience is rather large.

2. *Some teachers and trainers use panel groups*, each of which serves as a panel. In this approach, teachers and leaders divide a large group into sub-groups of three to six. Each sub-group or "panel" researches a problem, which it later discusses as a panel before the other group members. On a predetermined schedule each sub-group then serves as a panel.

3. *We can use a leadership team with the panel*. Generally, a leadership team consists of the moderator, recorder, a resource person, and a process observer. When called upon the recorder assists the moderator by reviewing the data presented by panel members. The resource person verifies facts and gives expert opinion when called upon. The process observer assists the moderator in evaluating how panelists work together. Some teachers and leaders find it helpful to seat the recorder, resource person, and process observer at a separate table in front of the group.

4. *Sometimes we use the dramatized panel*. The panel members wear costumes and discuss the problem in an appropriate setting.

5. *In the dispersed panel,* panel members stand at strategic places in the audience. This approach promotes still further the "feeling of popular participation.

Effective Moderators Promote Meaningful Discussion

1. Effective moderators *lead in planning discussion outlines in advance.* For example, one panel group decided upon the following problems to discuss in the area of leader training: What are some accepted patterns of leader training? What are advantages and disadvantages of in-service training programs? Should we establish an internship program for training leaders? How can we most economically go about establishing a leader training?

2. Effective moderators *state the problem clearly.* John Dewey said, "A problem well defined is half solved." Albert Einstein said, "The mere formulation of a problem is far more often essential than its solution."

3. Moderators *establish a casual, conversational climate*—but they avoid overdoing it!

4. Good moderators *brief the panel members on what to expect of the audience.* Panel members need to know something about such audience characteristics as educational and cultural backgrounds.

5. Tactful moderators *balance the talkative and nontalkative members.* Sometimes nontalkative members find it difficult to get a word in edgewise. The alert moderator seeks to balance the opportunity for response.

6. Effective moderators *prevent rabbit chasing*—or if you prefer a more sophisticated term, they prevent tangential meandering.

7. Good moderators both *encourage and practice objectivity.* They avoid taking sides. Some moderators find it difficult to hide their own prejudices.

8. An effective moderator *spreads audience participation.* In a large group he encourages participation from persons throughout the room—the back, the front; the left, the right.

9. A good moderator *leads the generalizer to be specific.* Of the person who says, "All youth are rebels," he asks in essence, "Name one!"

10. A skillful moderator *wears many hats.* Among his many roles he is Mr. Peacemaker

Mr. Prober
Mr. Clarifier
Mr. Navigator
Mr. Decentralizer
Mr. Summarizer
Mr. Relaxer.

As Mr. Peacemaker, he reconciles emotional conflicts. As Mr. Prober, he gets to the bottom of things. He learns to ask, Why? As Mr. Clarifier, he brings things into clear focus when ambiguity sets in. As Mr. Navigator, he guides the panel through such hazards as tangential meandering, time limitations, and too much emphasis on pet topics and nonessentials. In short he clears the way and navigates toward a goal.

He is Mr. Decentralizer, that is, he decentralizes conversation when conversation "cliques" begin to develop. Sometimes he can decentralize rather simply by saying something such as, "John, let's hear you evaluate Joe's proposal."

He is Mr. Summarizer. Periodically he summarizes the group's progress in the light of the discussion problem.

He is Mr. Relaxer. He has the ability to relieve tensions with an appropriate story or anecdote. One moderator, in summarizing progress, said "At this point on problem three, we have said *nothing!*" Then he assumed the role of Mr. Relaxer and continued with, "And speaking of nothing, did you hear the definition of nothing? Nothing is a pair of rimless glasses without lens worn by the little man who wasn't there to read between the lines of unwritten law."

We Can Combine the Panel with Other Methods

1. Most teachers and trainers use *the forum* with the panel. In the panel-forum, audience members participate by asking questions of the panelists or by making relevant and helpful comments.

2. We can ask *small study groups* to react to a panel or to prepare questions for a forum. Small study groups (or buzz groups) could also formulate problem statements for use by a panel.

3. *Listening teams* focus one's intent to learn. A moderator who uses listening teams along with the panel could make an assignment such as this: "Group 1 will listen for points of agreement among the panelists; group 2 will listen for points of disagreement."

4. We can present *case studies* for panel members to analyze.

In this instance, audience members should also have in hand a copy of the case.

5. Panel members and audience alike respond to problems presented through the *role play*. Role-players act out a problem situation observed by the audience and the panel members. The panel members then discuss the problems involved.

6. When time permits, panel members can use the steps in *problem solving* as a guide (get the facts, fit the facts together, suggest possible solutions, select best solutions, take action).

Effective Panel Members Follow Guidelines Too

1. A panel member must *know his subject*. His first three qualifications are:

(1) He must have something to say!

(2) He must have something to say!!

(3) He must have something to say!!!

As someone has wisely said, a panel member "can no more talk about what he doesn't know than come back from where he hasn't been!"

2. Good panelists *limit their remarks appropriately*. Most panel members could well heed the "kiss" formula.

      Keep

      It

      Short and simple (but sufficient),

      Stupid!

3. Good panelists *talk without prodding*. They can maintain proper balance between talkativeness and restraint. "Let each one serve the group to the measure of his endowment, as helpful managers of God's richly varied grace" (1 Peter 4:10, Berkeley).

4. Effective panelists *avoid irrelevant ideas*. They avoid needless leadups and explanations of what they intend to say.

5. Effective panel members *organize their ideas*. It helps when presenting several ideas to begin with "The first of three ideas is . . ."

6. Thoughtful panel members *avoid technical terms*. Try to analyze this statement: "You have committed a fallacy of alternatives, not exhaustive in the disjunctive form of the syllogism."

7. Panel members *play even more roles than the moderator*.

As Mr. Information Giver, he might say "I read the other day that . . ."

As Mr. Relaxer, he might say, "Did you hear the story about the man who . . . ?" As Mr. Evaluator he might say, "We've already achieved two of our goals fairly satisfactorily; but I feel we have not done so well on this problem." As Mr. Prober he might say, "But *why?* What do you mean by that?" As Mr. Information Seeker he might say, "Who recalls the population of Dallas?"

As Mr. Summarizer, he might say, "Up to this point we have said that . . ."

As Mr. Clarifier he might say, "I believe that Harry really meant that. . . ."

As Mr. Encourager, we can hear him say, "I appreciate John's good preparation for this discussion." As Mr. Mediator we can hear him reconciling points of view by saying, "Perhaps we are not as far apart as it appears . . ." As Mr. Navigator we can hear him keeping the conversation on the subject, "All of this sounds good, but could we look again at our discussion problem?"

As Mr. Decentralizer he might say, "John, from your experience you may be able to interpret for Raymond . . ."

8. The best of panel members must learn to admit "I just don't know"—at times.

The Audience Needs Guidelines Too

1. *Write out the questions* for the forum. Writing the questions out helps the inquirer to (1) keep 'em short!; (2) say clearly what he means; (3) avoid needless genealogies; (4) deal with essential issues; and (5) clarify his own thinking.

2. *Wait for recognition* from the moderator. Sooner or later he'll get the signal.

3. *Keep to the primary issues.* Avoid wasting time on "molehill" issues. Some people deserve the epitaph, "I fretted and fussed and pushed and shoved, looking for molehills to make mountains uv."

4. Address the moderator first, even when specifying a particular panel member.

Conclusion

Panels often change passive pupils into purposeful participants!— plan a panel.

124

Notes

[1] Kenneth L. Hoover, *Learning and Teaching in the Secondary School* (Boston: Allyn and Bacon, 1964), p. 125.

[2] Holbert and Gulley, *Discussion Conference and Group Process* (New York: Henry Holt and Company, 1960), p. 36.

[3] William M. Sattler and N. Edd Miller, *Discussion and Conference* (New York: Prentice-Hall, 1968).

[4] A. Craig Baird, *Discussion, Principles, and Types* (New York: McGraw-Hill, 1943), p. 197.

[5] James D. Williams, *Guiding Adults* (Nashville: Convention Press, 1969), p. 78.

[6] Sarah Little, *Learning Together in the Christian Fellowship* (Richmond: John Knox Press, 1956), p. 47.

[7] Paul Bergevin and Dwight Morris, *Group Process for Adult Education* (Greenwich: Seabury Press, 1950), p. 21.